OUTSKIRTS

# outskirts

◄ Sue Goyette ➤

BRICK BOOKS

Library and Archives Canada Cataloguing in Publication

Goyette, Sue
    Outskirts / Sue Goyette.

Poems.
ISBN 978-1-926829-68-5

    I. Title.

PS8563.O934O98 2010    C811'.54    C2010-907674-5

Second Printing – August, 2011

We acknowledge the Canada Council for the Arts, the Government of Canada
through the Canada Book Fund, and the Ontario Arts Council for their support
of our publishing program.

The cover image is a painting by Laura Dawe.

The author photograph was taken by Robyn Murphy.

The type is Joanna. It was designed by Eric Gill and first cut at the Caslon
    Foundry, London, in 1930.

Cover design by Alan Siu

Internal typography: Robert Bringhurst Ltd.

Printed and bound by Sunville Printco Inc.

BRICK BOOKS
431 Boler Road, Box 20081
London, Ontario N6K 4G6

www.brickbooks.ca

# CONTENTS

*my darkness, my cherry tree*

# my darkness, my cherry tree

The boy moves like a long-necked creature, a horse or a giraffe. With the same arc of reach, a gracious hunger, he lunges in front of my car impervious to its heft. His body is wily and wired for adventure though the soft skin of him still nuzzles the woolen mammal of family. His father, a force across the street, watches. We are in a globe theatre rehearsing tragedy. There are no lines. We are poised to remember each other for an eternity of remorse.

Forgive this enterprise of engine and fuel. Forgive its pads and pedals. The beast in my hands has escaped and gone feral. Listen to me blame the weather with its curdled clouds and tidal surge. Listen to me say you came out of nowhere. Are you the child chosen to draw satellites raking their slow trench across the heavens? Are you the child chosen to draw water into jugs for the thirsty tribe? Or do you simply draw the level of video game that is the present challenge? The toadstools and the capes, the crooked mountains and the secret keys? Weren't you chosen to be treasure?

Later, I will drive through the town of Economy and think of the way you looked at me in that second. The joy of seeing your father slurred with sudden panic. But only in your eyes and only for that moment. Immediately it wavered and delight moved back in. And such a force of delight, how it spread, the opposite of shadow, its hands on the heavy back of time, pushing it, shoving it still to let you squeeze by.

by the smell of my son's old room, the battle fume between Peacho the hamster
and Lego pirates. The vapour of their souls entwined in a kind of territorial

clash of cedar shavings and carpet. The mist of neglected math books,
the algebra of disregard and doodle. And the common denominator: socks.

Rolled up sneaker sweat, the grub of toes. Underwear everywhere. And socks.
I miss the poster of the phases of the moon hanging over his pillow

like thought bubbles in the graphic novel he narrated, the waning moon
of high school. The inevitable bong, that lava light of bright ideas

and the munchies, then the long moon of a new silence.
How else can they leave, our boys, but slowly?

His hand on the small of some girl's back, behind him the ruins
of dirty plates caught in a late-night computer search for other life forms

and the iPod he left plugged in, a vein of song recharging.
He'd come home to eat, stand at the fridge and graze.

And graze. Often we'd pass each other in the morning, me waking,
him a walking ad for the somniferous. Hi, I'd say. Oh, yeah, he'd reply.

And I'd miss the boy then who coloured drawings of his stories
with blue that actually matched the inside fruit of the colour.

His enthusiastic grade one I love chicks — how he meant it, literally,
a plump exuberance of pale yellow feathers perched on top

of his exclamation mark. This is where I'd linger, not wanting to go
into my morning yet, the kettle's inevitable boil and outside,

at the feeder, starlings trying to bully the treasured birds away.

You mention your daughter. How she left for university. You may have said more.
Someone at the far end of the table is talking politics and doesn't notice. Someone

opens more wine, bread is cut. Two of us put down our forks. This kind of silence
stops chewing and stands on its hind legs to peer into our forests. It's heard something

move. Arrested, it stops breathing. It will moult any whispering until it's fully
fledged. We are listening. We lean toward your daughter and her suitcases,

her backpack with its please and thank yous of Canadian flags sewn on the flap.
We lean forward as if she's our daughter and there's a recital of daughters,

a lark of girls who've returned from their travels to sit now between us. And we lean
in towards you. A triad of mothers still sometimes waiting at the window. Who knew

it would all go so fast? Our girls and their pirouette of news, the best friends, the cute
boys; oh, the different weather system of moods and the winds that matched each

of them. You are swallowing the decades of her and cannot speak. Neither can I.
This is how they return, in the middle of a conversation, pieces of soft wood smoking

and, if we wait long enough, catching and burning in our throats. There's a new silence
then, that begins, again, to breathe. Its ears perked but its head lowered. The long

grasses around it are still and sifting the sounds of the city. We pick up our forks, our
eyes brimming, and reach for the platters, accept the bowls being offered.

I want to tell all the long bearded boys that I have a boy just like them. I have a boy and I imagine he too turns dance floors into a ricochet of minimum wage and dumpster diving, demolition derby in the size of a parking space shadowed by condos of parents and student loans, Superstore aprons and vibrating cellphones. I have a boy who dances. I want to tell the girls wearing black leather chaps with matching bras, poised to shove, to check and boulder, that I have a girl and though she closes her eyes when she twirls, I've seen her avalanche. The mosh pit is a boil of bodies and the singer is sliding down the banister of his voice, sending the screech of his descent directly into the mic as if it's a combination of girlfriend and government. I feel old. The floor is hard, the sneers sideways. When the singer falls back, his eyes closed, his hands holding the bird, the shark, the satellite at bay in his chest, all their hands reach up and carry him aloft like a gift or an offering. This is what I'm supposed to watch. I didn't know how it would happen, just that it would. My boy, my girl; a dance carried. And then gone.

The floor is wide-plank pine. The day is waning. The girl sits before her mother and recites a memorized poem. Outside, the mother can't help noticing the chickadees. They're smaller than the maple's leaves, bigger than the cherry's. The piano is silenced, the mourners have come. Outside the wind picks up like a muffled drum. She watches her girl look up at the ceiling, down to the floor. The room cups her like a lotus, her jasmine tea lends its white petals to the voice of her. He was my North, she says and then remembers. My South. She's memorized the irrevocable direction of loss, her hands with their rings and bangles are as still as stones. There is an appetite for this kind of sadness that will soon know better but for now it is her talk, it is her song. Oh love that should last and how she was wrong. The mother has rehearsed as well. For this moment or moments similar. And yet, at her cue, the silence that had cupped her daughter like a lotus chooses then to bloom.

My son insisted on the story of the bird asking the tractor if it was its mother. I took
everything personally. I set the clocks back very time I drank. Once, I opened the

washing machine in the middle of the rinse cycle and a force of water escaped like a
season; a compact month of spring that frothed the basement ecologically. That may

have been a dream, all those leaves. And who knew about the dolphins? We were young
and looked out windows while we opened cans of tuna. Our big fight was keeping the

squirrels out of the bird feeders and turning off the television. Good night and good luck
Super Mario. I consulted Dr. Spock and drank decaffeinated coffee. There was a secret

level to all of this but I hadn't collected enough feathers to get into it. The first time I saw
this ocean was like being at a zoo and catching a glimpse of beast disappearing into

foliage. It vanished behind houses and, in the city, skulked behind banks. Later, I'd watch
it take over the street like a herd trolling for more water. I'd call my son from the

yard and hold him close. What's that, he'd ask. Fog, I'd say, but that word never seemed
thirsty enough.

The new mothers are petting the giraffe neck of street lights,
cooing for more light. The streets are so unsafe.

And they're buckling up their tenderness. Oh the state
of the world! The new mothers have to attach umbrellas

to the things that move their children from here
to there. There is no more driving. The price of black ice

and yellow lights and gasoline. And the weather!
Fuck, the new mothers want to say. They have to wash their water

with water. The whole planet is at the window peering in
while the new mothers sit on the side of the bed.

They have to be wolves; they have to be golden-winged
warblers. Reminders, reminders.

They bury their phones for a minute of peace,
rendezvous to master Goodnight Moon

while the earth rings and rings beneath their feet.

## SNOW DAY (#14)

She spends the morning crushing strollers. The laundry
is up to her hips. She minces threats into whispers. Recycle!
Her love is for them all. There are no matching bookends.

The hours can climb out of their cribs. She puts a safety gate
between now and the morning of her death. Her terror
is teething. She still has time to defrost her father's

letters. Slow down, she tells the plans skidding down
the hallway. Her mother will need watering. She scours
her morning with salt. She lets the birds trace her hands

for their art project. There is no question about it,
she will organize a memory swap. The phone is a flashlight
into her silence. She tries icing her kids' boredom so it will

taste better. The birds keep coming to the door. The one
with the shovel does the talking. The clouds are delivery trucks
with more weather. She can remember when a season lasted

a season. Her sisters are melting and can no longer hunt.
She dumps an ice cube tray of potential into her drink.
She's not dancing she tells them, she's twirling.

The fridge is her first husband. She still has a cupboard full
of punchlines she's saving for dessert. She decides to sneak one.
Something about the only time his light came on. Unfortunately,

her brain is a sieve. And her hands are garden tools. She finds
herself raking through their screeches for the truth. Okay. He hit her
but then she bit him over the princess puppet. The judicial system

of puppetry requires child removal. Aw, they moan, deciding now
to be harmonious. She could make excuses but she doesn't have enough
sugar. Cut it out! she yells and yes, hands them the scissors. The birds

need some pulleys and will no longer look her in the eye. The windows
demand her counsel. She is at the end of her rope. Everything starts
with a little olive oil and an onion she says to no one in particular.

The kids demand a story and jump on her nerves. She may have lost
her keys but she refuses to lose her mind! She stands at the sink
and watches a hydrangea of soap bubbles disappear down the drain.

And the snow feasts on her. And until it learns to speak, its tongue is Valium
and licks her to sleep. The snow examines her then, fills her ears with a muddle

of soft words her father should have said. That old dog, that angry belt. The snow
is a godsend. A fairy tale. A blizzard of questions: are you the wolf who poisoned

her children in an apartment in the east end of Montreal or are you the last of the diving
birds who finds herself trapped with a husband under the thick ice season of the suburbs

in Bedford? We all look the same to it and when you boil it down, it really is just
embittered rain. Mon dieu. The lives we've lived. The drama. The snow, in these parts,

is part of the religion. The part of the religion that blindfolds the house and leads it out
into the woods, spins it around three times and dares it to find its way back.

Oh, our dizzy houses tramping past the same clump of trees all night, a defeat of closed
doors and windows and the cold draft of moon while we sleep and sleep and sleep.

The snow slides its hands up her legs in this dark theatre and wishes she'd put up a fight,
wishes she'd push it away. A little petulance, a little melt, like the old days. A little

what do you say we get out of these wet clothes. The snow is so old-fashioned,
so stuck in its time. And it's quite the trapper, its sugared snares already buried

in her mouth, unhinged and waiting for that first succulent word.

Is her breath feuding with its sister? Does her sweater smell like an argument
or an apology? The nests in her thoughts, have the hatchlings learned to fly?

And the forest in her throat, have the lost questions found their way out
of the words? Her hands, have they migrated south into the second to last

ceremony? Her feet, are they still tasting the soup or have they been set upon
the table silent as spoons? Is the snow a seance? Has it read the history

of its ancestors and is now trying to get in touch with its dead? If the field
is a coma of forgotten flowers, will it remember the vines of her footsteps?

Does this woman want to be found? Can we knot her son's younger voice
into a net and haul her up from the depths? This hour, does it have its back to us

or have its hands warmed? Is her husband's magnet true north, are his eyes
still working compasses? Her name, is it still recharged? And the sleeping field mice,

is there a way we can brew their dreams for clues? Should we taste
the owl's talons? Are you sure this woman wants to be found?

Her car keys, have they left an echo of the duet they sing with her house key,
her shed key, her key to the trunk in the basement and that small key,

the silver one for the red suitcase they sometimes shared? Are her keys still chiming?

And the snow is already spooning the wax of street-light halos onto her eyes.
Has already loosened the house from around her neck. Oh the snow is a crooner,

glinting like Vegas, all chapel and hurry. The snow is on top of her like a new husband or
a dead husband; a weight, say, of something in between. The snow is laying down

tracks, a new way out. It's a hallelujah of yahoo prancing around its feast
like a ceremony. Then the snow is a priest to the great silence and bows at its altar

before putting its gospel to its lips and drinking. Grateful. Grateful.
The snow was married to the moon but things didn't work out and now this. This speed

dating, this love at first sight. In all of the hullabaloo, the snow has forgotten
to turn down her furnace, forgotten to turn out her lights. We've all done that, right?

Too tired to get up then the furnace kicks on, the room heats up and something melts
and costs us a little more. And isn't a name something that burns, like a piece of coal?

The way it can be tossed up into the night sky like a mute star and doesn't it always land
in our furnace? Burning us awake. Her name, her name pitched high, follows its old

migration path to where she secretly never stopped burning and when she opens her eyes,
it's the snow she sees first then the hot hands of something reminding her

of the holiest of protests.

Every morning a boy walks by my house, the neighbour's dog barks,
and this boy barks back. Which drives the dog crazy. I imagine it standing

on its hind legs at the window startled by the audacity, the New World accent,
the lack of proper credentials. The dog barks and its teeth snap,

saliva drools. Its collar cinches. The boy digs into his bark to where sound
is darker, he blows out his name and becomes, for a moment, a voice rising to meet

another threatened voice. Then he goes to school. And this is how a friendship
begins. The dog, for the rest of the morning, circles its pillow. Adjusts the blanket

and pulls the rubber octopus from under the couch. It does its work. Patrolling
the forest of chair legs. Trolling beneath the cabinets. A sentry up the stairs

then back down. Trouble simmers far off on the city's back burner. It scratches
behind its ear fervently, it cleans between its nails. Once in a while, it woofs

at something indiscernible, it growls. Waiting. When it sleeps, the boy climbs into
its dream and tries to steal its ball but the dog is mightier and its kingdom of balls

remains intact. Down the street, the boy at school runs ferociously, his wide arms plow
the wind out of his way. At recess he is starving and bites the head off his granola bar.

When he sits to spell his words, his legs move as if he's dreaming of running
or being chased.

## COURAGE

The seniors bring heavy spoons to their lips. They have committees
for setting the tables, for carrying the bowls. They sit next to each other

and wonder about snow removal, their winter coats lining the hallway
hunkered like husks. My mother doesn't drink but, to give this speech,

has downed a shot of vodka. Sylvia is in charge of many things, she begins.
You'd think at this age they'd notice the hive of souls they're sitting in,

the rasp of wings, the fingers not prying but recollecting by touch.
Sylvia bristles and sits up. The restaurant for the Christmas party has not been

reserved yet and vodka is the pirate taking over my mother's voice. Courage.
She is standing at the helm of the luncheon about to announce mutiny.

Who can blame her? Everything that dies in this small town flies its way
to these gatherings: the hollowed names of husbands and their resurrected

cardigans; the pilgrimages their wives make to the kitchen in the long mirage
of morning. In this leftover light, Sylvia stands up. She has things under control,

she tells them. And the ghosts of the bossy girls face one another, faded
and fragile-boned. They've become sisters in the back seat of the long drive.

They may as well be fighting over the window, the clear view of fields
giving over to sky. As long as they don't look up, as long as they keep each other

occupied until they get there. In this way they're saving themselves
from the bother, the business of being afraid. And from the last bewilderment

they'll feel when they finally do arrive at whatever comes after.

We got mad at the boys swimming next door. Incorrigible.
Unbelievable. Hooligans. They splashed. They ran from the deck

tarzanning into the July afternoon, yodeling a fierce pleasure
before bombing the pool water as far as it could go. Without them

the scene was pastoral. A quiet backyard gathering. But what did we want?
The world sometimes is a big wet dog shaking itself, the wag of trees,

the slobber of clouds. The little bark of bad news, of illness. We wanted to push it
off our laps, command it to sit, to stay. Obey, obey. The boys threw Doritos

at us. They howled. Finally one of us got up, went over to the fence. For fuck's sake.
Can't you? Will you please? The pool water reached you

and we watched the linen of your dress give over to white bra and then
to nipple. What did we want? Life but not with a mind of its own.

We wanted the kind of reverential hush a healing demands. A happy ending
you could walk into, bequeathed with more time, bearing angel food cake, stepping off

the deck into the green expanse of all you had left.

He saw me as I was leaving the restaurant but I saw you. Haunting him. You were the greenest plant, wide, succulent leaves dipped into the last of the light as if you were drinking it. You weren't the flowers in the dark but that one hanging over his table, a lingering begonia. You were the knife that cut his meal and the fork that placed it in his mouth. Nourishing such necessary talk. You were the nautical theme that surrounded him and his date, ocean and high waters, sailing vessels and indiscernible horizons. You are still his fear of drowning, his sunken treasure. The hidden navigational star, you're his lesson on forgiveness, dying the way you did; you, the master class on letting go, are his forward motion. The last time we talked was in this restaurant, in the slim corridor behind the stage while he sang to a room full without you. Now you're defying past tense and are still here, watching him go on. Ah, coaxing him closer by urging him away. His yes is so essential to her. Lined with your fur, your sigh, your purr: inevitably yes. And your voice, a bell past ringing, still praises.

My fingers were numb and all I could hear was someone yelling for help. The night had feasted on plums and aluminum. The boat was my childhood and it had turned over.

Later, after travelling with an outlaw of trees, I came to a clearing. The tallest pine had tipped the night to its lips. Call it a drinking problem or call it a vista. I sat and listened

to myself breathe. The rocks I was throwing turned into years; somewhere a phone rang and when I picked it up, my daughter's voice: Where are you? You said you'd be here.

And in that way, she was born. This is when the night began eating darker trees and roads. She insisted on going out anyway. The key around her neck shone like a happy

ending. I'm alright with the happy, it's the ending that keeps me in my chair. Yes, I began to tip the sky to my lips. It was a thirst spurred with stars. Swallowing the moon

was like swallowing the perfect thing to say. It nested in my throat dreaming of wings and a second chance. I began to sleep with the night. At first we had nothing in

common. We'd meet and undress quickly. I had never done anything like this before. It wore me out and soon I grew pale, listless. My doctor prescribed anything arboreal.

Try and stay green, she'd urge. Face your mother twice a day but stop drinking her sighs. There was a series of winters like a Canadian museum, painting after painting of snow.

Of light in snow. Plows clearing snow. It took me a decade to thaw. When I think about those winters now, it isn't a mountain covered in snow but my mother. When did you

become part of the landscape, I want to ask, but she would just shift the way mountains do, a long shrug that takes centuries.

OBITUARY

My father spoke, silenced his sorrow with the back of his hand, came away stuttering.

My father sat, exhausted his wife with the claw of his serenade, came away generated.

My father stood, tamed his lumber with the sedation of his chisel, came away beleafed.

My father slept, dreamt his forest with the song of his feet, came away immobilized.

My father woke, whittled his story with the jackknife of his anger, came away sawdust.

My father ate, dismantled his hour with the tool box of his dismay, came away puzzled.

My father lingered, aged his window with the has-been of winter, came away hungrier.

My father left, closed his family with the door of his portrait, came away still-lifed.

# IT'S NOT KEENING, IT IS A KIND OF HUNGER

I had swallowed a bird whole, that's what people thought. I tried telling them
that no, I hadn't swallowed a bird, I just didn't feel like talking

and the feathers coming out of my mouth were just a kind of silence, billowing.
When moths started coming out of my mouth, they thought I'd been a room

with a door closed for decades and now opening. In a way, they were right
but not about the door. I'm not a room, I wrote in a note I'd give

to whoever asked. My father has just died and the moths are the years
of silence between us finally taking wing. Yes, you could say an opening.

They'd step closer to me then, their hand reaching for my arm, my shoulder.
Oh, they'd say, your father. And he'd appear then, between us,

an urban river, smokestack or an eight lane expressway to cross. My father.
The clouds, the day he died, were sweaters draped over the shoulders

of the soft hills I looked to. The weather, maternal, tucking me in
and bringing me cool cloths for my forehead. I unfolded the chart

of the continent I'd just walked and was exhausted. All my clothes heaped
in the hamper, the animals set loose, the tinderbox dropped into the edge

of the Atlantic. This happens after a long journey, no? Every step you've taken,
every long shadow, each road appears briefly to bow before retiring.

*Are you okay, people ask, and when I open my mouth an ocean pours out,*
*not a postcard ocean, but a real one, with cold-blooded creatures skulking*

*at the bottom, their hunger on a separate hunt moving farther from their mouths.*

How could I forget you? Or even better: I have forgotten you. Celebrate. Your name is no longer on my tongue but dissolves like sugar in the water I drink. The moon has smoothed the snow. The sun has dried the rain. There is no sign of you. Ah the sorrow of sitting alone on the edge of a bed without a hand on your shoulder is no longer yours. The empty night and the needle of moon no longer find you. They no longer look. The breath you take is the slight breeze that pushes water against rock. The shade of the elm is an ease you can no longer claim and yet when I sit here, it is with you. Have you become every tree? Is that a cloud of you? Tell me when I look out over water to the wavering line of horizon, is it the length of you stretched out, sunning on the big rock of here, resting? You are wildly absent, yes, and everywhere.

*Who can blame you? Who can blame you?* Forgive the hands that sacrificed ceremony, the hands that dipped into the river and returned with a desire for a darker depth and for capture. Forgive the cold hands that scrabbled out from winter hungry, with snow on their heels. The hands on fire, the cupped and digging hands. Forgive the industrialized hands and the cowards. Forgive the hooks that once had been hands. Forgive the chimney and the sweeping hands. The commandeering hands. Forgive the suicide hands, the hands that threw, that pulled, that pushed. Forgive the hands that locked, that unlocked, that waved goodbye from the platform until you disappeared. Until you disappeared. Begin again. Beneath this tree. Its branch, your shoulder and a touch that requests nothing. Begin again beneath this tree and my hands; these branches, your shoulder, welcoming.

*And so, in my father, might not the girl have been hurriedly forging the key of her own lock?*

*And so, in my mother, might not the girl have been hurriedly hunting the terror of her own animal?*

*And so, in my children, might not the girl have been hurriedly polishing the stars of her own girl?*

*And so, in my fear, might not the girl have been hurriedly planting the high-rise of her own death?*

*And so, in my heart, might not the girl have been hurriedly gathering the pollen of her own blooming?*

*And so, in my confusion, might not the girl have been hurriedly rescheduling the shadow of her own orbit?*

*And so, in my solitude, might not the girl have been hurriedly loosening the harness of her own hurry?*

*And so, in my kitchen, might not the girl have been hurriedly steeping the leaves of her own name?*

*And so, in my city, might not the girl have been hurriedly planning the construction of her own waterfront?*

And so, in my woods, might not the girl have been hurriedly burning the grandmother of her own tree?

And so, in my sleep, might not the girl have been hurriedly dreaming the prediction of her own shine?

# INTRODUCING THE TREE: A LATHER OF GREEN

They'll sell you thousands of greens. Veronese green and emerald green and cadmium green and any sort of green you like; but that particular green, never. — PABLO PICASSO

This tired traveller has come to a stop. Its pachyderm of thoughts have evolved so completely it takes a whole season to unrest. The days of herd are over. This is a singular beast, watering in front of our house, wary of weather and this new air-conditioned heat. If you put your ear to its flank, you will hear a river of its history, a sorrow of tables and chairs and the movement north compassed to its moon. Its escapade is worthy of a choir of the slow-movers among us, the tortoises, the snails, the stones. But don't forget its lineage. Its shade is a time capsule; the continent of its silhouette has lured explorers from their beds. Though it's faint, its voice breathes jungle and the verdant labyrinth of lush. Diplomacy to the birds who have audience with its eyes. Forgiveness to the dogs, those urban taggers. It loves morning best. No, it loves evening. This is the least of its arguments. It is unnamed in the truest sense. I have seen its sisters fall and only then, in their giving over, have I heard that green. Unforgettable.

Come over here and see for yourself. The grass isn't as green as it looks. Think of the poor Chinese poet surrounded by huts and other poets who had candles and bowls and pennies to buy lilies. How he walked every day, his job the dumb herding of unhurried cows through clover and the industry of bees. Read how he carried a bamboo stick for the flies and for the poems that would appear like the next dance, bowing deeply and him acquiescing, writing what he could on the back of a cow, its brown spots like a country for his words. O, he had his days of sitting on his rock, ignoring the dynasty of clouds dragoning over his head. He had his days of looking at his feet. He'd talk to the cows and their solar system eyes, wishing for another world, a world with a chair and a table in the soft light of blossoms, a pot of tea, a fan, a cat for company. He'd wish for a mat to sleep on, a wife with strong and soft hands. An audience.

Come over and sit in this grass. Look, there are ants and small black beetles eating the earth blade by blade; listen, the whirring is the same. Distance is the greatest con. Somewhere there was a man with a shadow of his heart scratched onto the back of a cow. The sky was above him, below him, his feet. When he finished writing one poem, he moved to the next cow. His days were long, the grass sweet. He had no idea what was about to happen. There were a great many cows in his herd; they'd stand patiently, his stick scratching the right spot. And this, we should know, is enough.

## BAD DINNER GUEST, BAD


The monologue about the deer is followed by the exclamation
of weight gain then the reminiscent travelogue about the trip

to the old hardware store near the fire station. Not to be confused
by the new hardware store closer to the church, which strikes her as funny

and if we wanted to, we could count her molars when she laughs. Ah, dentistry.
But onto the counting of the sheep! Literally. The neighbour at her cottage

has sheep. We're falling asleep but she rouses us, her fist on the table,
declaring she should keep chickens. Splendid idea, a lark of a thought, she thinks

and wonders about a rooster. A rudester, she says, cock-a-doodling so early
and someone passes the salad around again. The lettuce is limp, or suicidal,

throwing itself against my potatoes or washing onto them like a survivor.
Breathless. She doesn't watch TV. And she doesn't diet but they are making pants

smaller aren't they? She will not buy anything online or give out
her credit card number. Her partner fixed her hard drive and she has decided

not to dye her hair. Oh, she knows about the latest research, but it's the environment,
apparently we have fucked everything. Pass the butter, pass the salt.

Foolish how we still take the bait of her questions like old-fashioned fish.
She doesn't think they'll ever come back. The fish. There is a government

to overturn and dessert to be doled out. There is no question about ice cream
with the crumble. Blueberry. And we all must have it.

Even the cloud next to it is more of a cloud; the rain tucked
in its folds like napping babies, a cutlery of lightning

polished in its scullery. The cloud next to that one
has its door closed but is inside hunched over a drawing board,

the palm trees of its imagination bending to the streets
where everyone is screaming and running for cover.

But the one over my house looks like a small lap dog, eager
to please, the toughness buffed off it, its patina the pale white

of a pushover. The cloud over my house is a failure of a cloud
that won't even wisp along with the rest of the crowd and when it has its chance —

when, for a moment, it is caught in the rays of the setting sun,
for example, or someone from down here stops to point it out — it refuses

to be the shape of a party hat or a rhinoceros, it is bashful
and insists it knows nothing about weather, that it hasn't prepared.

Go on without me, it demurs, and then becomes a quiet puff
of brood when the sky actually does.

The fly that hovers above the old cat is too early. The cat
is just sleeping. I had to get on my knees to check.

The fly got in when the door was open to the gossip of two men
looking for work. They've pared their living down to knapsacks

and are prepared to pick strawberries or shovel dirt. The fly
surfed their laughter and landed in the living room above the cat

like a satellite or a vulture depending on who you're reading.
I'm reading Faulkner so the fly has a seven-foot wingspan

and can spot death's brother measuring the sleeping length of the cat
for its travels. Later, after the men leave, I tell the cat

there are sardines for lunch. The fly is our doomed plans
and their sinking shovel, the fly is an escaped tombstone

and the humming hymn of sooner, by and by, or later. Everything
is unwinding this summer. The wheelbarrow is filled with the fallen

flowers of the thorned black locust. When you hold the bills
out like a bouquet, I can hear the front porch in your voice

and the dust of the season rising beyond it like debt.
And when the cat yawns we both hear the purred dreams

of the missing gold piled high, counting both the heads
and tails of our breath.

If you play the Jazz at Massey Hall CD, be prepared: Parker and Gillespie had been stranded at the airport and their swing still swarms with junkie desperation. That desperation is orphaned now and will move in with your thoughts. And the autographed Cohen, a wedding present, will divorce you from all hopes of Cohen prowess in the rooms of the house you were once best in. I do not say this lightly, we haven't met, you and I, but your hands squirrelled through my underwear drawer and that, my friend, must count as something. Have you heard how life is somehow

balanced? The caterpillars and new birds and the synchronicity of their hatching? Appetite and survival? You kicked in my door and somehow your door will now be opened as well. There is no way to prepare for any of this. In the deep coffin between songs, you'll hear your mother whisper forgiveness. Forgive the chain gang of puns, your recurring dream of termites asking: Is the bar tender here? Is the bar tender here? I am new at the urban curse; I've mostly worked with tenacious crows early in the undeveloped morning. The Rod Stewart CD, his greatest hits? The anchor of my good taste that I hope, hot legs, will somehow manage to sink you.

O ladder, it is twilight and the wire connecting the bulbs has disappeared, even you are slowly dissolving. He is aloft, among the trees with an armful of light, cascading souls of sparrows, illuminated notes of the melodic minor spilling between his hands. Twilight has its back to us and there is a convoy of lit cells, those holy messengers to the street-light, to the sky. Little fish, phosphorescent kisses, a halo of tongues. There once were so many trees, we couldn't see the forest for them. Remember the fear of being lost? The woods ready for one big swallow? He is standing up among the trees as if,

as if he is one of them, a ripe offering. His voice lifts and I am a light. Have I ever loved this much? The house behind me, all of its rooms, its open doorways, stacks of plates, its clutch of spoons. Whoever has no house now, come in, come in. Listen: it is an autumn evening. Things have changed. If I am to believe my eyes, there is a man hovering in the branches beyond the cherry tree holding out a bouquet like a marriage. There is nothing standing between us, soon this darkness will lap even us up. Soon there will just be those lights.

For those of us who must first picture a map of Canada before venturing off in a set direction, let's stay close together. History is often based on a wrong turn and there are great catastrophes looming. Fortunately, we have other skills. The way we navigate through the city by its trees. Tell us to turn toward the birch that quivers in the last light and then walk the moonlit side of Citadel Hill and we'd get there, guided by the sky curdled with low clouds. We don't get lost,

we are the disciples of the side-tracked, surveyors of the grand scheme around the corner. We have antennae and don't need to ask for help. Farms look familiar. The lilac at the corner across from the barber's is half-way there. We have seen that fire hydrant painted as a dragon before. We worship at our private altars lit up for the Intuitive. Our way is the right way. A short cut. Trust us. The only longitude we know is the breadth of degrees and minutes apart. It's when we see each other, our loves, you and I, company on this dark journey, this caravan of homes; it's then that our hearts, those old dogs, wag in recognition. Found, we exclaim, we rejoice. We've been found.

For all of us who cannot hold a note, who cannot hear the piano-wire spine of a tune and sing anyway. Sociable. May we all raise our glasses. Let us hope we continue to misinterpret the looks of surprise as silent praise. Never mind that we're strapped to the song like a muffler on a '79 Buick, never mind the precious tuning forks, the plug-in tuners, the metronomes. Minor chords aren't really that major. Forget about the diaphragm and that whole business of breathing. We are the special choir who isn't satisfied by conversation, and the planet needs us: wingless birds, skyless clouds, oh tender warblers. Were we the early kids at the park, verging on the operatic while being shoved off high things? Oui, merci, we'd say, not having a clue. We are such an agreeable bunch, oh masterful diplomats shouting the chorus, taking the lyrics and ripping them off with our teeth, our hearts beating in battle-cry unison.

We are the wild altars, beats in front of the drumming, steps ahead of the rest of the tribe.

The raspberries are so ripe, pick is too strong a word.
The only thing keeping them real are their seeds
and these scratches. There are sharp knives in the air

slicing away the city, and the berries thicken the song
with red notes. In the next field, one cow braves
the hill while the others beseech it not to. So far,

no sight of the ocean. Lately it's been stalking us,
appearing silently behind the trees. Beyond the newspaper box
on Barrington. It's a relief to be away from that look it gives.

The farmer's daughter is a dress rehearsal and solar-powered.
If there are sharp knives in the air, she is trying
to convince them to cut her free. How old is she, thirteen,

fourteen? Sure the squash flowers are lovely but talk about
metamorphosis! The coltish legs of her beauty aren't yet strong
enough to hold her. Childhood is a brief moon in a blue sky;

the start of the day in the company of its ending. She tells us
what we owe and there is a tenderness to this moment. Later,
in photographs, it will look like the trees are growing right out of her.

When the farmer speaks, the earth softens and the swallows nudge
their fledglings from his mouth. He has lined the hard headlines
with feathers and is nesting on the hope that his fields will go on

without him. Hunger is a rocky soil that sifts through the hours
before dawn and there has always been an acreage of doubts
weeding his fields. Some come to pick berries and some are tempted

by the trampoline in the yard. Others heft the fallen tools by the barn
as a measure of their own strength. Either way, persistence
is an early crop and this man has been up before dawn.

*We're sorry we're so sorry but we are sorry. It's a Canadian thing like tourtière or Irving. Picture a moose trudging through tundra towards another moose, antlers grazing maple trees that haven't been cut down yet, the snort of exertion, the clomp of intent. That's us trying to find each other in this wilderness so we can apologize for something: standing too close, standing too far. Being hard to find in the appointment thicket of our days. We're sorry one of us invented frozen fish fillets because single-portion frozen dinners invented a new loneliness and the lonely bone, they say, is connected to the drinking bone. The rest, well, the rest is history.*

*Our apologies are welcome mats and engagement rings. The tiebreaker in overtime. Pierre Berton's bow ties. Meaningful. We take an eternity to back into a parking spot and then feel sorry for all the unparked cars still circling; we're even sorry for feeling a little lucky. And though having a pocketful of loonies is a good thing here, it sounds like something we should apologize for. We roll up the rim to win at the same place we see Jesus miraged on the wall beside the drive-thru window. We are sorry though for our ehs, our toques, about/aboot. We're sorry for the poutine (but not for our beer or Leonard Cohen). We tap our trees and drink from them. We understand then what it's like to blossom though we don't speak of this. The sky is such a choir here.*

*We're sorry how scared we get when our love sees its own shadow, how we disappear for a long season. We wish we could but often, we can't. Désolé, désolé, we try. Our apologies are foghorns in the great sea of social gatherings where we pass each other like tankers gliding by the shore of an all-you-can-eat buffet. I am truly sorry for that last line. The poet John Thompson said we are brave at our kitchen tables, brave in our beds but cowards under the moon. We are sorry for that as well. The moon has a way of calling us out from our homes and we stand beneath its whiteness, stripped of nerve. The trees are an endangered silence then, witnessing. Winter is a mystery. The night breathes us in and waits for what we have to say for ourselves. The shift must happen now. Transformation. Our apologies braver, migrating into the realm of reprieve when we hear ourselves say:* forgive us and then what can we do?

We will meet at Gus's pub. In the darkest corner. We will gamble.

We will lose everything and then convince each other that losing is a winning experience.

We will be reminded to pay for our beers and will only have lighters. We've quit smoking but will not brag, will not say anything about poverty, that last weathered apple.

We will be asked to leave and will convince each other that leaving was our idea.

We will build a fire and sit around it. Halifax, we'll agree, is a hard-haunted town. The ghost of green, a long ago season.

We will not think silence is a takeover or we're in any way cheap labour. A winter without slush won't break our backs. It may be global warming but it isn't warm.

We will not say anything when a stranger says: trees are fence enough.

We will breathe that one in like a community.

We will put our hands on his forehead and conclude he's suffering from homesickness.

We will admit we're all suffering. Oh home away from home. Oh trees. Oh planet.

We will agree to do something. We'll compose a letter and then borrow a bike in this preposterous January, this winterless winter.

We will find our legs by riding the bike around the fire until the flames get greedy and snap like a shark.

*We will want revenge and will burn our hands. The stranger will have to be carried. We will not complain of how heavy he is. He spoke of trees; he spoke of trees!*

*Our courage will flail then. The night so endangered.* 9-1-1, 9-1-1!: *it is the dead of winter and we can no longer see our breath. Rumours bruise our resolve. A car is alarming.*

*It will be up to us. We'll have to knock on neighbours' doors, we'll have to wake them. No, really. We will have to wake them up. Then we'll have to run.*

# the last animal

We shouldn't have set the heart of the night on fire.

— RENÉ CHAR

## fog

Fog is nomadic. A low prowl of Atlantic rooting
through the city like a bear. In the small town of Prospect,

fog once swallowed a school bus. The children,
taught to hold hands in an emergency, emerged older

and craving gills. Fog is a flood of the moonlight souls
of dead fishermen. The elders warned us not to breathe it in

or we'd cough for days, their last thoughts caught in the net
of our lungs. Watch how fog seduces a lamppost. It's a crowded harem

vying to undress all lights. It can turn a thought into a pigeon,
the bird that refuses to be unwelcomed and keeps coming back

and keeps coming back. Fog is the migrating breath
that careens off mirrors; it's smoke from the fire of our names

that the ocean keeps putting out. A travelling salesman for thirst,
it's got a briefcase squalled with gulls. It's the Mafioso of wind

coming to collect its street corners and the mastermind behind
getting lost. It swallows directions and small cries for help,

spitting out the bones of life jackets. It puts its snout against our windows
and breathes heavily, the succulent smell of home, a feast it's starving for

in the middle of its clouded travels. The lit shark fins of taxis swim
through streets as meaningfully as the coast guard but fog has a mouthful

of rocks and a swarm of blind hands. When it finds you, it's been said,
it will chew you in a way that you'll not soon forget and will linger

like a shell to your ear, convincing you the answers
to your many questions all sound like the ocean.

AQUIFERS


one


So far receptive yearning has found there are close to 100,000 cubic wistfuls
of music hidden in the aquifers across the country — a large, rich supply.

But most of them are echoes that were trapped underground long ago
by the bewildered rainfall of the broken-hearted or the lost. Happiness

can be replenished but grows more slowly than previously believed
and most voices don't drill very deep. We may run out of music —

echoes are just voice shadows and will not quench our thirst. Up until now,
Canada has had little information about how much underground music it has,

how we are recharged and when it all may run out.

two


Gathering is important because the human voice taps our agricultural roots
and constructs a subdivision of voice that affects the heart of our supplies.

Any kind of concert is really useful because it helps us sing our need.
Just how long must we sing? Study the aquifer of joy! Especially laughing,

that ribbon of voice and song that peals through silence like an alarm clock.
The excavation, which started in 2003, aims to douse the daily news

with a groundswell of voices across the country's headlines.
By listening and monitoring our thirsty ears, researchers can measure

the speed and direction of the flow of music within the radius
of our work weeks. They are also examining the layers of memory

and grief in our voices that will influence the irrigation of loss in the area.
The study has spent a million contaminants of past grievances to gather data

on our twelve purest intentions.

three


Music will be used to develop a topography of happiness
that decision-makers can use to forecast the effect of vocal range

in the brief dark, in the noise extraction of silence
and in the emotional climate change on awkward family members

dancing nonetheless. The last time Canada conducted a national singing study
was in 1967, before professional listening was invented and before families

had access to instruments such as the soprano of cellphones
and the airborne geoharmonics of hearts texting. We really need to know

in some detail where this music flows so that we can drill
for other potential sources of wonder to deplete global malaise

and the contamination of our worried thirst. Our lack of understanding
has posed a challenge in areas such as universities, where students,

originating as rain or snow, rely on studying and have scarce dance supplies.

four


We are worried about new high-density neighbours
behind our properties. The municipality said it has allowed

this new development to go ahead and raise its ruckus
based on a study that shows there is enough silence

for a new subdivision of disharmonies. Conservation measures
to protect silence must be taken. However, silence has been largely

blacked out, allegedly to protect the privacy of the families yelling
and to prevent singing from gaining a competitive advantage

over discord. We're concerned because we already run out of joy
if we do five loads of laundry and the dishes in sequence.

Joy levels in our submersible backyards also dwindle
when our neighbours harvest their fights. Everything is tied together!

We just don't exactly know how or where! Study the ecology
and biochemistry of the northern reservoirs of laughter in the watershed

of family photos. We precipitate such a source
of important information when we cry!

five


*We really need to know in some detail how our joy flows*
*and in which direction it goes so that we can divine*

*and then drink it. Potential threats that deplete or contaminate*
*it should be redirected. Warning! There are hangovers from karaoke!*

*Such as a curfew of enforced silence, a headache of critical ears,*
*ridicule and a shortage of the endangered words of amour. Center Canada*

*around this new climate change, happiness can grow exponentially!*
*Severe singing shortages are still possible unless decision-makers*

*gain access to enriched kitchen parties. Drill for your own voice!*

## fog

Fog is polishing the street on its hands and knees.
There is a forehead of mailboxes. A throat of street lights.

Your one thought is hunting with sharp teeth and keeps jumping
the back of your sleep until it bleeds. So now you're awake.

The plans you make involve freeing a trapped rescue plan
and raising awareness of the eroding shoreline between sleeping

and this wakefulness. Some, you've read, have actually moved their beds
farther from the sea. Some are bringing sleep in by the milligram

and wedging support beams up against their dreams. But still.
You're awake in a city bridged to another city with a serpent of water

between them. If you are to trust your eyes, you've aged,
and the window is nothing but the trees of your childhood

reflected on your face, the street light a jewel in the middle
of your forehead. Who knew what you'd grow into?

There were opinions. Those who heard you sing lingered
in doorways to hear more and thought you were destined

to doctor the wings of unmigrated wounds. Others, who tasted your soup,
believed you to be a light brightening the darkness of strangers.

Your name, with the right shoreline, is the original harbour
for home. This city you chose is up to its balconies in the heavy breath

of ocean. Sleep is retreating and, in the marsh around midnight, it's you
who's standing in the hallway, watching windows pronounce this new era

with their sudden lights, melting.

Sleep is retreating. Migrating landward. In extreme cases,

disappearing. The construction of new dreams may need

an expensive foothold of large apologies. The rising levels

of ring tones may force the shorelines of silence over the top.

It's best to obtain older vertical air photos of your family

before buying any new ideas. The slumping on our faces

cuts into the dune line of our resolve. Our bones are melting

offshore! There must be a safe setback for mystery

if our children plan on using this property after we're gone.

Night isn't the only undependable glacial melt; the ocean

never repeats itself.

Holophote action occurs when light strikes the sleeper's face,

compressing memory in the cracks of the dream. This puts

tremendous pressure on the surrounding marriage. The light

then expands explosively, forcing out pieces of exhaustion.

Over time, the sleeper's mouth opens, sometimes forming

a cave. The dream which was removed falls to the bottom of the heart's

seabed and is used for another night of action. (Attrition and Corrasion)


Resistance occurs when sleep grinds dreams together,

causing them to become smoother and reduced in size. As sleep

rocks from side to side it moves the dreams causing pieces of dream

to become reduced in colour, argument and violence. As well as colliding

with other dreams, the dream also collides with the sleeper's heartbase

causing pieces of coralloid memory to break off the base of the sleeper's

heart contributing to this wakeful action. (Abrasion)

Corrasion occurs when breathing breaks in the sleeper, pounding

the sleeper and slowly eroding her. As sleep pounds the sleeper

it also uses the dream of the singing mother from other dreams

to batter and break off pieces of the sleeper's heart from higher up

the cliff of memory, which can be used for this same breathless panic. (Attrition)


Remorse or resolution occurs when the pH balance of sleep's current

corrodes the dreams in the sleeper. Usually the sleepers to be greatly

eroded in this manner are sensitive sleepers who have a high pH level

of ocean in their blood. The rocking action of sleep also increases the rate

of reaction or remorse by removing the reacted marriage, the singing parent

or the ocean from the sleeper's blood.

fog: forgotten names begin their journey home

In our hurry, haven't we all mistakenly called our last-born
by the dog's name? And haven't we, in a mortified moment,

called our husband, our wife that long ago name from an era
of brief sunlight in apartment windows and humid, twisted bed sheets?

What did you think would happen to those misplaced names
we sing out, the ember of them burning small holes in the silence

that breaks with the indignant I am not the dog!
The wrong names don't take wing or even wheels

but are a kind of embarrassed exhaust that steams
our early mornings so when we stand at our counters

biding the kettle's climb, the trees that have been there forever
are misted with the migrating orphanage of their company.

EROSION

one

Erosion is the process by which darkness is removed from cliffs

and beaches, causing the duskline to retreat inland. It is a natural process

that provides an argument for building better coastal nights.

*Waves and currents transport the nocturnal, its silence and dreams,*

*to adjacent shores such as ancient family photos and barrier reefs*

*of the missing, offshore, into basins of warm water memories*

*and seabeds where the clamshells of our hearts reside, thereby resupplying*

*and maintaining the marshes around our solitude.*

Erosion is a very serious process in the evolution of our coastally emotional

landscapes. However, erosion can be a hazard. If our shoreline

of solitude continues to erode or if homes, businesses and public buildings

are situated too close to the present shoreline of oceanic wilderness,

they can be undermined with the unresolved. At times,

especially during severe emotional squalls, erosion can even damage

the wharves, sea walls and breakwaters that were built to protect

the coastal seabed of our clamshell hearts, nestled so deep

and at sea.

two

Many people cause erosion when they drive from excuse to

diversion during the evening. In most regions, the pounding of headlights

on the duskline, during an outbreak of hurry, is an important concern.

Headlights attack at the base of a road and scatter untamed possibilities,

exposing the deeper potential of family to erosion. If there is insufficient

singing to replace the busy schedule of our nighttime, the darkness

will retreat or change shape so that it can better maintain its kingdom

against bright disagreements and the natural process of heartbreak. A gale

of mistrust causes erosion of dancing and handholding from homes,

but music is often returned to the kitchen during fair weather.

Another important cause of erosion is a rise in anger which exposes

career choice to a current attack. If insufficient spirit is added to the coast

of our biographies during a rise in the memory level, the rate of joy inland

will likely decrease.

three

The short answer is "ice," but it was caused by two different effects,

both of which are visible in our parents' tidal tempers. More than

10,000 years ago, marriages were largely under the influence of an Ice

Age. Most of the northern disagreements were covered by an obstinacy

kilometres thick. This stubbornness had formed from fear of not being

appreciated, and of death. In the process, the level of trust dropped by more

than 100 metres. As the Ice Age came to an end and tempers began to

melt, families were returned to the oceans of days, which again began

to rise. To a small extent, families are still swimming, and can be perceived

in areas such as Nova Scotia.

four

In Canada, where many families were to be found during the Ice Age,

another factor is important: the weight of our ambition on the Earth's crust.

With career paths now grown-over, the ocean is rebounding

to its original position. Escaping from the resulting work week,

coastlining tourists can be found in the Arctic of their lives,

where lightweight cameras and cellphones make the sea level appear

to be dropping, instead of swallowing them whole. There is one further

factor to be considered: because we are adding large volumes of unrest

and other gases into the atmosphere, chimney sweeps estimate that aggression

is beginning to heat up faster as a result of the low-threshold effect.

The low-threshold effect may be eating the melting rate of the remaining hope

in the hibernating winter. In addition warm feelings take up more room

than cold ones so if our hearts warm, they will expand. The prediction is that the unknown will start to rise at a faster rate over the next century, and that many areas of Canada and the rest of the world will be subjected to accelerated rates of coastal confusion.

five


Pressures of conflicting uses of night are expected to increase

over the coming years. In order to allow for better design of dark hours

and more responsible cavorting of coastal communities, it is necessary

to understand the geological and oceanographic process of heartache operating

beneath us. Understanding the physical framework of this despair and the response

of a particular full moon to the natural process of wanting to talk will help

prevent costly errors in long-distance drunken phone calls

by locating local structures and facilities in the coastal zone that can be trusted,

and will greatly reduce our vulnerability to erosion.

six

Emotional protection can be a very expensive business because of the cost

of forgiveness and trust reconstruction and the ongoing maintenance

as memory levels rise. But it can be done

in order to protect important belief installations such as

self as leader, self as life of the party, ports, and mayor of all opinions.

In many cases where parades were planned in the past,

the present has proven less than an adequate celebration.

With the increased risk of nocturnal erosion posed by demand warming,

there is a greater need than ever for Canada to understand

everything, to adapt to the rising level of the misconstrued

and to manage the development of our own private coastlines

that have tried to remain in the dark.

seven


Recent monitoring of two nights on the Eastern Shore of Nova Scotia

has shown the differences in the ability to commit: one low pebble-cobble

argument migrated 100 metres landward into a kitchen between 1996 and 2006,

whereas a higher pebble-cobble argument a few houses away shows

little retreat. Obviously, in families where the arguments are silent

the rate of retreat is barely noticeable over genealogical time.

In louder areas, where the families are composed of loose cannons,

gravel voices and reputational mud, the rate of retreat is much higher.

In Atlantic Canada, rates of retreat can reach out for the police

and voices may travel up to 10 metres per year, but generally

less than one metre per year if drinking is done in moderation.

Historical records show the loss of entire marriages along the coast

of Nova Scotia. Closer to the ocean, the average rate of retreat is generally higher, between full moons and high tides

where ten kilograms of broken dishes are reported per year.

eight

Despair removal from the foreshore of our nights is dependant

on the power of our voices crossing our arguments. This plea must reach

a mediated pitch or remain a whisper told up close. On any night, whispers

can be very persistent and may take many years to completely disappear.

Slowing down dissipates manic energy on the foreshore of our evenings

and can provide a proposal of protection to our sleep from eroding worry.

If our voices are not lowered, the darkness must widen

and become more effective at dissipating arguments so that fewer

and less important conversations can reach our beds. The depth of our love

is so close to shore. It can be measured by lowering our voices

to the bottom of our beds and watching the current of our words find

each other's lips shh-ing into a kiss that pulls the tide in full.

GETTING IN THE OCEAN

Don't trust it. Your feet may test it, but it's doing the tasting.
I've heard people complain, if you're not there at feeding time,

all it does is sleep. I most admire the headlong dives.
As if its immensity were penetrable. Sure, we can hold our breath

but then what are we swimming against? I never know what to call it.
The French have a pronoun for everything. The night and the moon

are sisters; the ocean, the quiet stranger they're so hot for.
What they don't tell us in tourist books is how we tried catching it,

the trickery with floodlights, the soft lisp of wharves. When farmers visit
the beach, all they see is another field being plowed. When carpenters visit,

they want to straighten the lifeguard tower. Children believe they're at
a reunion. Every summer, there's a safari of beachgoers gawking to catch

a glimpse of tail and fins. The photographers set up for days. Their diaries
evolving into complaint: We've been out here for over a month

and all we can see are waves. It's kind of a housing project,
one city dweller exclaimed, spearing his beach umbrella into his shadow.

We haven't seen the half of it but will get down on our knees
only if we lose a flip-flop. If you've ever fallen asleep next to it, you know

how symbiosis works, the predatory shark of dreams with their double row
of teeth and the expanse of sleep that barely manages to return us

back to shore.

## A.K.A. THE FOGHORN

The people living in those new condos near the'harbour
aren't complaining about the foghorn, they're complaining

because, really, the ocean transgresses, forgets its place
and sends its tentacles out into the city to eat its lights

and tender shoes. The bellow is thick and salted, the long
throat of the drowned and the small clams of their hearts

spurred into its riptide. What they're worried about,
those condo dwellers, is how the sound comes warning

under the door, seeps into windows and sharks their sleep,
swimming with an open mouth and swallowing everything

in its path, filtering their dreams for the sweet larva
of memory. What they're really complaining about is how

they're forgetting the small squid of names they once sustained
and how the ones who named them are inevitably going under.

The longshore drift of Halifax traffic

is corroding the face of conversations and creating

the birth of small caves. The lunar current is an abrasion

on both bridges. City lights are starving

the night of its sands. Shadows, generated by a storm

of darkness, may take the form of long-term

loss of rocks and sentiment. A temporary

redistribution of foreshores will enliven

the beach parties so necessary after the long work week.

Everywhere, across the land, weekends were washed away

overnight! Haligonians woke to overturned Mondays

and had to pull in their nets, the last of their dreams,

phosphorescent but out of water and barely breathing.

Halifax, the capital of the medieval fog trade,

is nonetheless enduring.

one

Few wet depressions or aspects of a deciduous anxiety have roots

on the landscape as far-reaching as this new-growth fear. Over 95% of questions

harvested in Nova Scotia are answered using the technique of clear-cutting.

Clear-cutting a question involves cutting down virtually every standing curiosity

in a given neighbourhood, leaving an exposed heartland of vulnerable limbs

and tire ruts where a rich shady child once stood. Between 1975 and 1999,

almost 10,000 kilometres of Nova Scotian curiosity was slashed and burned,

which is more than a sixth of all the ideas in the province, and almost a quarter

of the exclamation marks and eurekas. (!!)

two

The habitat of Nova Scotia old growth conversations has been greatly degraded

by 400 years of privacy pirating, opinion redevelopment and, more recently,

texting. Over the past two decades of conversing, the rate of interrupting

has doubled in volume endangering all acoustic confessions.

In the last decade alone, the number of conversations thinned annually at supper tables

has doubled to almost 70,000 hectares of television and website soliloquies.

In Nova Scotia, almost all misunderstandings (98%) are accomplished

by hurried speeches or similar even-voiced managed reprimands.

Over the last 40 years, the percentage of Nova Scotia fathers older than 80 years

has fallen from 25% to just one percent. And women older than 100 years

have become reduced to scattered groves representing less than one half percent

of the shade of our mothers.

three

Conversations occur on both private and public benches. Almost 80%

of provincially owned public benches are unprotected, and most of these

conversations are wastelands of burned silence. Once conversations are clear-cut,

they are forever altered. Some lowlands of voice will grow a herbaceous layer

of politeness, but there will be fewer tender words with fewer plurals to grow on,

less singing from plant and animal species, less anchorage from the elders,

and no breeze at all from prayer.

four

Artificial conversation starters often encourage one or two seedlings of mild insult

and veiled accusation over a hardwood of compliments to initiate exchanges.

This creates a single species of silence, a monoculture of hard feelings

that share the same weight and size. This even-thrown monoculture is far less operatic

than the natural multi-voiced (or uneven-aged) family brawl of the supper table,

and these silences support a community of simmering unrest. Considering the aim

of a Protected Conversation Network is to support bio "diversities," it becomes clear

that charcoals of silence and the mistrust they create are not consistent with the aims

of protecting Nova Scotia's wild heritage of rhetoric, tall tales, and outright,

but interesting, false claims.

five


Two centuries of riving old growth silence and logging curiosity have severely

degraded Nova Scotia's natural wealth of imagination. 99% of inspiration

in the province is an aloof sawmill. Nova Scotia has lost nearly all its old

forest bread crumbs within the last 40 years. A 1958 survey

found 25% of the province's homes still dominated by stories

more than 80 years old. Today, just over one percent of our wolves

are that seductive. There has also been a sharp reduction in valuable species

like apologies, requests, mysteries and monsters as well as a virtual extinction of flirting.

Heritage flirting in Nova Scotia is endangered and exists in very small,

scattered, isolated bars in the carbon sink of the province. The volume

of loneliness in Nova Scotia has doubled over the past two decades.

Most opportunities for quaking aspen have been clear-cut with the contempt

of an Ice Age. The current annual rate of speed dating is both aerobically

and emotionally unsustainable.

six

The changes taking place have sharply forgotten the value

of Nova Scotia foreplay due to:

- the loss of the caressable verbs
- the loss of a large radius of invitations and clear thoughts that fetch premium company
- the loss of resistance to first person infestation that results from species bragging
- the loss of recreational adjectives that can impact lovemaking
- a decline in listening that is likely contributing to a 50% decline in shade-dependent passionate innuendos.

The Gross Domestic Product gives no value to blushing,

and thus counts fumbling for the right word and barely talking above a whisper

as production loss. This is bad accounting, like a tree selling off its shade

and counting it as profit. Current debatable accounting methods ignore the loss

of non-debatable values such as preserving proposals, the ecology of first words,

noun diversity, awkward erosion, broadleaf understanding, the non-fertility

of stoic silence and the preservation of shade in the bright glare of possibility.

Local protesters claim the situation may be turned around

by providing greater incentives for investment in the root system

of worn-in jokes, greenhousing ideas, protection of initial shyness

and other spontaneous social hijinks and instant good-natured calamities.

seven

Indiscriminant interrupting is based on the idea that meaning is louder

that way. By interrupting, we plow the conversation

so much that what was once a unique proposal loses its appeal.

It can be a challenge to tell people to listen when love may be involved.

But restoration of heartwood silence should be key. We don't listen to hear;

we look at the person to see what they're selling. Once you hear

the macropores in a conversation and realize all the conduits its forest protects,

you should stop your pillaging. Branches and their small cones

are more important than getting out of our grass skirts.

If we can get the transpirational leaves of our whispers in synch

with the thirsty leaves of our loneliness, the rains will come.

But if we rake all the dry whispers up, we'll lose the rain

and will become more susceptible to lonely with a capital Why Me?

eight

*We should start planting words that are most likely to survive should warming*

*trends continue. Soft words suitable for such warm climates include*

sarmentosal fingers *and* aboreal kissing, *while* arguments, hostility,

relationship issues *and* ruinous drinking *should be avoided. Hard words*

*likely to survive in warmer temperatures are the inventive words*

like jazzypants *and* orchestral orgasms. *Meanwhile the* feud,

*the* excuse *and the* rivalry *are more likely to die out if warming trends*

*continue.* Enchanting, awe *and* mesmerizing *are species*

*that are predicted to be suitable in the future. A rule of thumb is:*

*if the word is planed north of the mouth, in the headland region,*

*it probably doesn't have much warm temperature potential.*

*If it's planed in the south, the heartland region, it probably does.*

*This conference of days is an opportunity to slow dance*

with the latest research in the canopy of forests, and to harvest

ourselves on the best practices by listening to expert trees pioneering

in this new neighbourhood of love.

## fog

It's the ocean, listening. It watches you rub your forehead and look
back at it. It presses against the trees until you can no longer see

your neighbours. Now, you're an island. And you probably have
something to say. Ah, the patience of a continent. Like it has all the time

in the world. Further out in the city the bridge has disappeared.
Cars approach the ramp and, for a second, hesitate before crossing.

This was not meaningful until you watched your friend die. Her hesitation
and then her inevitable slow move across. You want to be able to say

something about this. How lately, she is the haunt of your thoughts. Behind you
there is a room full of people meeting a new baby. The children run through

the hallways as if they're the motor that's keeping all of you going. Last year's
leaves are barely letting the crocuses through. Soon you'll rake. And soon

the ocean will recede back to itself with the song of your breathing still in its hands.

You will not have time to hesitate. Aim for the ripe side of the hour
with the tranquilizer gun then fix your sights on the lean minutes

stalking the river. You may have started off berry picking but how quickly
things have changed! If you don't have a tranquilizer gun

then use your body to get between it and your child.
Remember the mantra: minutes only feel like teeth. Minutes

only feel like teeth. Your child will have a berry-smeared mouth.
She will want to know what's making her wet. Hey, she'll say,

what is that that's making me wet? Your voice will sparrow
to her. Rain, you'll hear yourself say and then before you know it,

it will make its move. Hey, she'll say again, rolling under it.
This is when hesitation is no longer an option. Those of us older than you

sometimes hesitated; we couldn't believe what was right in front of us.
Time was different then, it wasn't so traffic-jammed, so prevention-treated.

It wasn't over-fished. Time then was kind of a loner, walking the streets
like a stranger without a map. We didn't have to practice our breathing

or balance on the moment of it like a log. We often fell into the dark
hours like a lake, but we learned to swim. We burned our fingers

lighting fires. They say it's starving now, how once it's caught you can get close enough to count its ribs. But no one can remember it hunting

like this before. The crouch of its hunger so ready to spring.

The light of the moon ricochets off the bulrushes and projects itself into a moose. Your foot on the brake is doing mouth to mouth. C'mon. The minute is overweight and

sweaty. All you see is a wonderment of nonchalance. This beast has swallowed the woods and is transporting them across the highway. You hunch, convinced you could

drive under it. You hunch because you're facing something both horny and holy. Doesn't everything important start with that same impulse? Your heart in the passenger seat

needs its asthma pump. Have you seen its asthma pump? Your heart in the booster seat kicks the back of your seat: Are we there yet? The night is looking out the window at

its own reflection. You call out to your angels, you pray for giant cartoon hands to pull this moment from its bones. This is how you were raised. Desperate. You are not in

good shape and now you are skidding. Up close the moose is an elegance of scraggle and you succumb. To die with this new idea of beauty. The car is a curtsy before everything

wild on a trespass of highway. And you are the chosen apology. Your hands loosen. When you look back up to it, it's no longer there, and days later: was it ever?

The night waded into the ocean. Up to its waist, it looked back to us on shore. Its look was morose and someone said: Why is it going out so far? One of us stood and waved.

Its shoulders drooped as if carrying the stones it had collected all day back into the water, as if carrying the weight of the world. None of us saw it actually go under. We were

asked later, pressed into remembering. We'd been drinking. There had been an argument about who actually said what. It's like you neglected your own child, someone said

thumping his fist. I thought it was a moose, someone finally confessed. It moved like a moose, with those long strides, head and shoulders above caring about any of us.

Someone else had been reminded of her father, it had the same gait of him leaving the house for the office. Who am I, someone else said, who am I to stop anyone from doing

what they want to do? Once it was in the water, it seeped into everything. The pines and spruce at the edge of the inlet, the cabin on the other side of the dunes. The harbour

further along the shore was a rebellion of small-fisted lights. We lit a fire and waited for it to wade back out. Someone walked the water's edge with a flashlight. We might have

better luck, someone said, if we even knew what to call it.

It was like the ocean had escaped. *A house cat disappeared. And then a lone walker.* We stood on the sidewalks and wondered what we could do. One of us had inherited a gun.

It doesn't have any bullets but no one else has to know that, he said. *Someone's phone rang, its ring tone a fury of crows.* One of us saw it behind their shed. *It looked like it*

was eating something, she said, and we all looked down and were quiet. I think it's a herd of something. *No, it's travelling alone.* We promised to call if we heard anything. *There*

were more sightings. *Under the bridge. A fire left burning on the hill.* Someone's mother felt it come up behind her in the kitchen. *Relentless.* Hard times call for hard

measures, one of us said. *We were young. Trees were umbrellas then, open and shading us from the rain.* Maybe we're looking at this all wrong, one of us said. *Shh.*

Some nights the moon was spectacular, poised between two planets, other nights it was just a rind of itself. *This is how many of us felt, spectacular and then just a rind of*

ourselves. Is anyone else dreaming of it, someone asked. *It was the beginning of a new century. The era of fast rivers.* The minutes set sail, sloshing against the hard rock of

each hour. *And the city shopped like gulls fishing the far horizon.* We were lulled by the sound of our days hitting the shore, the consumer motion of their rise and then fall. *Night*

was the real ocean. *In this way, years passed. But then.* What was it that stepped from me to drink from those dark hours? *All we could do was watch.* The cupped hands and

the thirst. Is this, one of us asked, how we'll finally get to know it?

Here is the shadow of one small child. Here is the warmth from beneath
the sleeping cat. Here is the recorded breath from a rushed phone message

apologizing. Here is my daughter's bike. No, not my daughter.
Here is an oven mitt and a can opener. Here is the linden tree

hungover from drinking an entire collection of slow-moving seasons.
Here are the headlights of a car heading for the hospital.

Here is the baying of fear, and the coyote of awake. Here is a year
of routine. Here is saved gift wrap and string. Here is the teenage bellow

of boys, their hearts full moons demanding more sky. Here is the cloud
that resembles a small god lying with its back to us. Here is an hour of rain

and here is the thirst of anything captured. Here is my father's cough.
Here is a reading lamp and an address book of rivers. Here is an obituary

for a forest. Here is a briefcase full of diaries. Here is a suit to wear
to the trial. Here are small scissors to trim your hems. Here is a mirror.

Here is a photograph someone took of you when you weren't looking. Here is
memory pressed between pages, its petals translucent and dim.

Here are the promised jewels. Is that enough? We swim the channels
of your long hours so easily, and you, you hungry ocean,

when did you start being so tempted to keep us?

## THIS LAST LAMP

Do not be deceived: this last lamp does not give more light – the dark has only become more absorbed in itself. — PAUL CELAN

Like the deer running erratic in the mall, the dark is out of breath. It's not that you're chasing it, more like holding up torches and threatening to. It's good weather for a witch

hunt and you don't trust it, do you? This last lamp is held up to examine the dark tongue of animal. What has it eaten and how does it talk? This last lamp is a miner down the

long throat of midnight. Your father sits with his thermos, his legs not being what they used to be. Go on without me, he says, and you do. What choice do you have but to

strike his gentle words like a match? The only thing that burns is the lonely hour without him. Ah, grown up, how do you tell the time? There is a wolf in your memory; when

you wake, you see it running with something in its mouth. Save the children, your wife screams, and you get out of bed and start the car before realizing it was only a dream.

The children are long gone, the stilt of their shadows, a high-rise towering over the rural plot you've become, you a scruff of ragweed and thistle. Remember your plans? And the

candle you called yourself?

To go in the dark with a light is to know the light.
To know the dark, go dark.
— WENDELL BERRY

*We dissolved in you like sugar and had no choice but to hunt for galaxies. Our hands disappeared in front of us. Planets, we were told, are one constant light; open for*

*business. Have we always been too big for our boots? We forgot to ask what exactly you do. Do you fill trees with your shadow, blue leaves starched in moon? Is that your*

*secret? Or do you urge them to branch out, an earth-filled mouthful? There was so much to explore. We were young and thought you were ours. We thought everything was.*

*We entered you like a cave. With flashlights. Our voices flailed like bats. Such grand adventurers. Such spotlights. No one bothered with your name.*

*There was a specialist with a device but in the end he simply put his ear to you and listened. Oh, I suppose we got bored. You were like a dying whale in the harbour,*

*just lying there. We'd kick but you wouldn't flinch. Someone had a knife and a family to feed. You know the story. We had you surrounded and you didn't put up a fight.*

Now that we have you, tell us: how many have you hidden? Who do you most desire to bruise? Alibi, alibi, how do you tell time? Oh voracious appetite, who will you lose

next? The sounds sacrificed at your altar, do you hear them? Are you the blindfold or the legion of questions? The border to cross or the refugee crossing it? Do you kneel

before relinquishing the sky or leave it crawling, dusty as a miner? Those jewels, are they your teeth or your crown? How far will you flee? And these searchlights, do they burn?

It's no longer simple. We pack the car and drive to you like a destination. Out of the city. Farther than the suburbs. The last of you is hunted and you sit far from the road.

When we do find you, you're feral and suspicious. Who can blame you? We hold out our hands and you eat them. You've been trapped; bayonets, blades, scythes of light.

You're a hulk of wound cornered. When the stars shoot, we're surprised at how stellular we feel. Ooh, we say. Aah. The kingdom of you waking. Trees must swallow river-

hinge to turn that colour. Grass must be trampled by an equinox of rain to sound so green. When you finally stand, we're blind for a moment; lanterns for the soft glow of

wanting more.

Darkness is the last animal. We hold out moonflowers and tender welcomes. Ignore the condos and their balcony halos, the street lights hunched with concern. There is an

exodus of us craving its redemptive waters. Gladly we will unclothe and submerge, steep until we feel it in our veins. There's no use any longer denying that it's a part of us.

Banished one, come home. It's time we speak to our deaths as brethren. You have learned to walk in step so well you're silent. Yet any minute your hand on our throats,

squeezing our hearts, may tighten.

Unmoor the last light. And stand on the shore. How often we watch something leave

for the last time without knowing it.

We cannot slow down to hear ourselves think. If we did, the great sadness

would descend and not leave for many winters. Yes, we'd learn to live with it.

And it would loosen its grip; the inevitable choice of watching

everything go. Patience. Darkness bears its own sight. The path is lit by the sound of

our footsteps.

¶ "Audition" uses lines from W.H. Auden's "Funeral Blues."

¶ "Obituary" relies on the form of a sentence from *The Elegance of the Hedgehog* by Muriel Barbery: *My father straightens, wipes his brow with the back of his sleeves, comes away home.*

¶ "Girl Gathering Girl" relies on the form of a sentence from "The Weaker Vessel" by Yasunari Kawabata: *And so, in my dream, might not the girl have been hurriedly gathering the shards of her own fall?*

¶ "Aquifers," "The Coastal Headlands of Our Sleep," "The Four Main Actions of Sleeplessness," "Erosion," "This Collapsed Section of Time" and "Clear-cut" are government and ecological texts reconsidered.

EPIGRAPHS

¶ René Char's quotation is from "On an Unadorned Night" (*John Thompson: Collected Poems and Translations*, edited by Peter Sanger, Goose Lane Editions). Paul Celan's quotation is from "Backlight" (*Collected Prose*, translated by Rosemarie Waldrop, Routledge). Wendell Berry's quotation is from "To Know the Dark" (*The Selected Poems*, Counterpoint Press).

¶ "Resist" was written in the company of René Char.

ACKNOWLEDGEMENTS

❡ Poems have appeared in *Grain, The Malahat Review, The Literary Review of Canada, Prism International, boulderpavement, Matrix, The Fiddlehead, The Best Canadian Poetry in English,* 2010 (Tightrope Books) and *enRoute Magazine.* A selection from *Outskirts* won the 2008 CBC Literary Award for Poetry, and "The New Mothers" won the 2010 Earle Birney Poetry Prize.

❡ Thanks to my family, friends, students and colleagues for their inextinguishable spirits and electric conversations. Thanks to Jan Zwicky, Alayna Munce, Kitty Lewis and Brick Books. Thanks also to Robert Bringhurst for wrangling my long lines. I'm grateful for the support from the Nova Scotia Department of Tourism, Culture & Heritage and the Canada Council for the Arts.

———

for Pete

BIOGRAPHICAL NOTE

Sue Goyette has published two books of poems, *The True Names of Birds* (Brick Books) and *Undone* (Brick Books), and has been nominated for the Governor General's Award, the Pat Lowther Award, the Gerald Lampert Award, the Atlantic Poetry Award, the Plantos/Acorn Award for Poetry and the Dartmouth Book Award. Her novel, *Lures* (HarperCollins), was short-listed for the Thomas Head Raddall Atlantic Fiction Award. She teaches creative writing at Dalhousie University. She also participates in the Writers' Federation of Nova Scotia's Mentorship and Writers in the Schools programs and has taught at Sage Hill, the Banff Centre Wired Writing Studio and the Blue Heron Workshop.

There is no camp. No ashes to shift. The patios are empty save the barbeques. More than a minute online is dangerous, especially if you've been drinking. Obsessive

whistling has got to stop, there is no longer any theme song. Everything is ninety percent advertisement patrolled by an army of shopping hours. Stay off the paths. Eat less, carry

more. The young ones bearing weapons will want to name the animals, dissuade them. If you are to count the cows, count also the plates. Steam rumours open and eat the nut

at their core. Leave the gossip to the rivers. Photographs will be buried at the base of diseased trees. All eyes are distractible, smiles are especially alluring. The sump pump

can't get rid of the water and god, I am told, is a canoe-shaped hole in all of us. Books, those old grandmothers, are losing their teeth. Stay focused. Those aren't stars, they're

flashlights. Add, don't divide. Love best those who have forgotten how. There are no favourites in this dark. Now scatter.